SOCIAL SECURITY BASICS

SOCIAL SECURITY BASICS

9 **Essentials**
That **Everyone** Should Know

Devin Carroll

DEDICATION

For my mom, Wanda Carroll,
for a life of selfless service and devotion to your family.

Acknowledgements

This book would not have been possible without the help of many people.

Thanks to my wife, Karen, for encouraging me to get this project finished. She also deserves an award for tolerating me as I often stared off into space thinking about my book when I should have been focusing on our conversation.

Thanks to my kids, Ethan, Lauren, and Hannah for listening to me ramble about Social Security (even though they are not remotely interested).

Thanks to my development team for making me look and sound polished: Kali Hawlk and Kate Horrel for your wordsmithing; Jim Blankenship for your technical review; Teddi Black for your patience in designing my cover art; and Megan McCullough for your ability to take a messed-up document and lay it out into a well-designed book.

And a huge thank you to the readers of my blog, SocialSecurityIntelligence.com for suggesting I write this book and being such great fans.

DISCLAIMER

This book is meant to be for educational and general information purposes only.

It does not provide specific tax, legal, or financial advice. Please consult with your own advisors for personalized advice around your specific situation.

This book, the author, or any of the related entities are not affiliated with or endorsed by the Social Security Administration or the US Government.

Praise for
Social Security Basics

"Social Security Basics is required reading for every elder law attorney in my firm."

John K. Ross IV - Elder law attorney and co-host of the Big Picture Retirement podcast

"This book is a wonderful reference guide for those looking for simple information or complex details from someone who knows their stuff!"

Andrew Comstock, CFA
- Owner, Castlebar Asset Management

"The rules relating to Social Security are long, complex, and dry. This book distills the most relevant parts into an understandable story that is easy to follow."

Brandon Renfro, Ph.D.
- Assistant Professor of Finance, ETBU

"Making decisions about Social Security benefits can be intimidating but it doesn't have to be. This is a fantastic book to explain what you really need to know."

David Waldrop, CFP - The Astute Advisor Blog and Bridgeview Capital Advisors

"Devin Carroll is the perfect person to untangle Social Security's mumbo-jumbo. He tells you plainly only those basics you need to know. During my 25 years working in finance, I've often wondered, 'Why hasn't someone listed the basics in one place?' Then I realized just how hard it was! That doesn't stop Devin. He makes the rules look simple, taking concepts most mess up and laying them out in an easy to understand format. Bravo!"

Joe Saul-Sehy, Stacking Benjamins Podcast Creator and Host

"Social Security is an important component of your comprehensive financial plan. Yet, even if you don't have a financial plan, there are still decisions you'll be faced with regarding Social Security that could have a financial impact for 25 or more years of your retirement. Devin's book, Social Security Basics, is an indispensable resource in helping you make smart, informed decisions about your Social Security benefits so you'll have a more confident and comfortable retirement ahead of you."

-Russ Thornton, WealthcareForWomen.com

"Devin Carroll is my go-to resource for all questions about Social Security. His in-depth knowledge and simple style of explaining things make it possible for anyone to understand the complex rules of Social Security benefits."

Kate Horrell, military family money expert

"Devin is the one I turn to for answers on complicated Social Security questions. He knows his stuff and explains things in an easy to understand way."

Roger P. Whitney, CFP®, CIMA®, CPWA®, AIF®, host of the award-winning Retirement Answer Man podcast

"Given so much complexity, Devin does a fantastic job distilling the Essentials that everyone must know to make good decisions about claiming Social Security benefits!"

Michael Kitces, Publisher, Nerd's Eye View at Kitces.com

About The Author

Devin Carroll is a financial planner who is obsessed with Social Security. To share what he learns with others, he launched Social Security Intelligence.com and his YouTube channel at Youtube.com/devincarroll.

His expertise in Social Security and retirement-related issues has been covered by numerous publications including Yahoo Finance, NASDAQ, PBS, Forbes, US News, AARP and several others.

He lives in Texarkana, Texas with his family.

Notes From The Author

There are plenty of books that offer a comprehensive examination of Social Security benefits.

That's not what this book is about.

In all the years I've spent writing and speaking on the topic, I've found that most of the questions I receive can be answered with a good knowledge of just 9 of the Social Security basics.

You don't need to do lots of painful studying or complex number-crunching to grasp the necessary concepts. Once you learn these basics, the rest of the Social Security system starts to make more sense.

I often compare this kind of planning to driving my car. I understand that if I press the accelerator, I'll move forward; I'll move faster. Understanding the intricacies of the car's internal combustion engine, however, is not necessary for me to perform this basic action and create forward movement. I understand that if I turn the steering wheel, my car will change direction. I don't need to know the precise workings of caster angles, steering linkages, or the variation of Ackermann steering geometry that my vehicle uses to use the steering wheel and successfully turn the car. In short, I have enough knowledge to keep me safe and allow me to perform the basic operations that I need.

That's the intent of this book: to provide the knowledge you need to successfully, safely, and accurately navigate the maze of Social Security with confidence.

This book could have been much larger and filled with extremely detailed, nuanced tidbits of information that may or may not apply to you. That's not the book I set out to author. Entire chapters ended up on the proverbial cutting room floor because they weren't critical pieces of knowledge you absolutely needed to understand Social Security.

What's left are the basics you need to know to help you make a smart filing decision. I wanted to offer you a book of essentials, and even more importantly, a book you could actually use. With that being said, I hope you find this book fulfills that promise for you.

.

Table of Contents

Chapter 1
Introduction

"Devin, why is Social Security so &#%!@ complicated?"

Under normal circumstances, my office walls don't hear much profanity or coarse language. That day was different. My client was hopping mad -- not at me, but at a screwed-up system that is often incomprehensible.

That system is Social Security, and in case you haven't yet gotten familiar with how confusing and contradictory its rules often are, it's not hard to find an example to show you. Take this excerpt from the handbook their technicians use for processing claims: *"We consider that an initial determination is correct even if we send an incorrect notice."*

Huh? What's that supposed to mean?

The Social Security rulebook is full of great examples of how *not* to write clearly. It's not completely the Social Security Administration's (or SSA's) fault, though. Over the last 80 years, Social Security evolved into something completely different from where it started. As it changed, new rules were written. As new rules were written, new explanations of those rules were added to the book. Today, the Social Security

Administration has two websites of more than 100,000 pages to help you understand those rules.

A huge rule book is not the SSA's only challenge. According to a recent Senate report, budget cuts have caused the agency to close 64 field offices just since 2010. The Social Security Administration has also shed some 11,000 workers and continues to cut back on in-person services. The solution to fewer employees but an increasing demand for the program? Send seniors and others to the 100,000-page website to conduct their business on their own.

This is some of what my angry client was dealing with. He was a widower who made multiple trips to the local Social Security office. He simply wanted a good explanation of how and why his benefit was being reduced the way it was. Unfortunately, it seemed no one could adequately explain it. He initially felt that his only option was to accept the reduced benefit payment they were telling him he would receive, even though he was pretty sure that reduction was too much.

But after stewing on it for a few days, he was ready for war. He changed his mind and decided there was no way he was simply going to accept what he was being told. He was convinced the answers were out there -- and he was determined to find them.

It took him a few phone calls and dead ends, but he finally found his way into my office. To make a long story a bit shorter, we were able to get him the answers he needed. As it turned out, his benefit was going to be cut more than he expected, but substantially less than he had been told at the Social Security Administration. And although the news wasn't exactly what he was hoping for, he wasn't cursing when he left.

There are *thousands* of people just like that client we helped. Baby boomers are filing applications for retirement and disability benefits in record numbers, but the SSA doesn't seem to have the resources to meet such demands. In 2013, more than 43 million people visited a Social Security field office. Phone service centers see massive amounts of overwhelming activity, too. In 2011, only 3% of callers to the Social Security Administration's 800 number received a busy signal. In 2014, it was nearly five times that number. For those fortunate enough to get through, the wait time was 17 minutes. That's three times higher than it was in 2012!

The Social Security Administration is quickly becoming like many other federal agencies such as the IRS: they have a public help line and some local offices -- but have you ever tried calling them? Have you ever tried to visit those offices? It's a mess.

To make matters a little bit worse, Social Security rules have gotten so complex that many of the technicians at the Social Security Administration don't fully understand them. There's a decent chance your financial advisor probably isn't going to be any help, either. A study by Nationwide Retirement Research found that among people 50 or older, only one in five received any advice on Social Security benefits from their financial advisor. When you add the Social Security Administration's reluctance to give specific advice, you can find yourself in a situation that feels nearly impossible to resolve.

Here's what all this means for you: the burden is on *you* to figure out Social Security, the benefits you can claim, and the best filing strategies to get those benefits.

Reading this book is an excellent first step to equip yourself with the knowledge you need. I'm glad you've picked it up and have read it this far. Many people in your situation believe the topic is simply too complex for them to learn and apply, so they never try or they just ignore the problem. But you *can* learn what you need to make informed decisions about Social Security.

This book will break down the complex big picture into digestible chapters that make the individual topics understandable. When you finish, you'll be a pro at Social Security.

Chapter 1 Takeaways

- If you want to make the most of your Social Security benefits, you need to learn the basics for yourself.

- That might sound daunting, but you *can* understand Social Security and gain working knowledge that allows you to make smart, informed decisions about your benefits.

Chapter 2

The Importance
of Social Security

Filing for Social Security could be one of the most important decisions of your retirement. What you know about the system and your benefits can make a huge impact on your financial life -- and can make the difference between meeting your needs later in life or falling short. Unfortunately, this is not an *easy* decision to make on your own.

According to the Social Security Administration, the average retired family receives 38% of their income from Social Security benefits. The amount of benefit income you receive may be higher or lower than average, but it's likely that your Social Security benefit will be your only income stream that:

- Adjusts most years for inflation.

- Is backed by the United States of America.

- Will pay you for as long as you live.

While all three of those benefits are great, an income stream that will pay you for as long as you live is possibly the best feature of Social Security. It's worth taking a close look at what this could mean for you and the retirement you want.

Social Security Provides Income for Life

Over the past 30 years, the responsibility of providing an income in your retirement years has gradually shifted away from your employer and squarely onto your shoulders. Pensions were once a fundamental part of an employee benefits package, but they're seldom offered today and are no longer a large part of the retirement income picture.

With most of the burden to provide an income stream throughout your family's lifetime on you, it's important that you maximize every opportunity and financial advantage you can to successfully generate the income streams you need to stay afloat. Your Social Security benefit can help in providing that income -- and even become income for life -- as well as offer your loved ones some protection against financial hardship once you pass away.

Clearly, getting your filing decision right when it comes to your Social Security benefits is crucial. In most cases, you only get one chance to get it right. If you make a mistake when filing for retirement benefits, it could cost you – and the loved ones you leave behind – thousands of dollars in missed benefits. So before you file, you need to do your homework.

The good news is that with the right guide, it doesn't have to be too hard. That's what I'm here to provide you with: a condensed, straightforward guide that starts you down the path of making sense of this convoluted system.

When I first started earnestly studying Social Security, the massive website and rulebook felt like I was drinking from a fire hose. It was just too much information! But after spending the last several years studying, speaking, and writing on Social Security, I've learned that most questions can be answered by learning the basics of Social Security.

So even if you feel you already have a firm grasp of some of these basic concepts, most of us could always benefit from at least a refresher, so I highly recommend reading through this book from front to back to make sure you don't miss a thing.

Chapter 2 Takeaways

- With the burden almost solely on you to generate the income you need for retirement, knowing how to maximize your Social Security benefit is critical knowledge for you and your loved ones.

- You generally don't get a second chance to get your filing strategy right -- so it's worth doing the legwork to ensure you file correctly the first time.

Chapter 3
Social Security Credits

Social Security credits are the building blocks that the Social Security Administration relies on to determine whether you qualify for one of its programs.

In 2021, you receive one credit for each $1,470 of earnings, up to the maximum of four credits per year. The amount of earnings needed to earn a credit increases annually as average wage levels increase. You can find more details, and look up the numbers that apply to your specific situation, on the Social Security website. One stipulation is that your earnings must be subject to Social Security tax to count for a credit.

In exchange for the tax you pay, you earn eligibility for the following important benefits:

- Social Security Retirement Benefits
- Social Security Disability Benefits
- Social Security Survivor Benefits

Each of these programs has different requirements for the number of credits to gain eligibility. We'll take a closer look at the specific benefits and programs in a moment. But first, let's cover the eligibility for each.

Credits for Retirement Benefits

The Social Security credits required for retirement benefits are the easiest to understand. If you were born after 1929, you must be "fully insured" for eligibility. This simply means that you have earned 40 credits. In most cases, all 40 credits can be satisfied by 10 years of work. If you do not have enough Social Security credits based on your work history, you may qualify for a benefit on a spouse's work record.

Credits for Survivor Benefits

Social Security survivor benefits do not always require you to be fully insured (40 credits). An individual who does not have 40 credits may still be eligible for survivor benefits if they are "currently insured." The Social Security Administration defines "currently insured" as having at least six Social Security credits during the full 13-quarter period ending with the calendar quarter in which the worker dies. This means that if you haven't yet worked for 10 years, your survivor may still be eligible for benefits if you have worked at least 1.5 years of the prior 3.25 years.

Credits for Disability Benefits

Generally, the number of Social Security credits required for disability benefits is 40. You must also have recent work history. In fact, 20 of your credits must have been earned in the last 10 years ending with the year you become disabled (unless you're blind). Simply put, this means that you need to have worked in 5 of the past 10 years. Since disabilities can also happen to younger workers, there are some except to the 40-credit rule.

The rules on disability are as follows:

- **If you become disabled prior to age 24:** If you earned six Social Security credits in the three year period (ending when your disability starts), you may qualify for benefits. These credits have to be earned in the three year period when your disability *starts*, not when you file for Social Security Disability Income (SSDI). If you become disabled and file a year later, the 12 month period while you were not working would not be counted as part of the three year period.

- **If you're disabled between the age of 24 to 31:** If you have Social Security credits for at least half of the time between age 21 and the time you are disabled, you could qualify for SSDI. For example, if you become disabled at age 26, you would need credit for two and a half years of work (10 credits) out of the past five years (between ages 21 and 26).

- **Age 31 or older:** At age 31, the rules for required credits are simplified. It begins with a requirement of 20 credits (between ages 31-42) and gradually increases thereafter. Generally, you need to have the number of Social Security credits shown in the chart below.

DISABILITY AGE	NEEDED SOCIAL SECURITY CREDITS
31-42	20
43	21
44	22
45	23
46	24
47	25
48	26
49	27
50	28
51	29
52	30
53	31
54	32
55	33
56	34
57	35
58	36
59	37
60	38
61	39
62 or older	40

What About Credits for Medicare?

Technically, there are no credits required for Medicare. The credits for Medicare simply reduce, or eliminate, your Medicare Part A premium. The chart below lists the Part A premium amounts for the corresponding Social Security credits.

CREDITS	PART A PREMIUM (2021)
Less than 30	$471
30 - 39	$259
40+	$0

There are a few other exceptions to receiving free Part A Medicare. As with retirement benefits, you may qualify for free Part A Medicare on a spouse's work record.

For Part B, everyone pays a premium. For most, it's $148.50 per month (in 2021). However, it's important to note that the premiums are higher for individuals over certain income amounts.

Medicare is a whole other beast of a government program to tackle, and getting into the weeds here is outside the scope of this book's purpose. But if you need more information, including the current year's premium amounts, you can head to Medicare's website at www.medicare.gov/.

Now that you understand how many credits you need, how confident are you that the number of credits reported on your Social Security earnings record is accurate? Unless you've checked it recently, you shouldn't be too sure. You can easily check your own earnings history by simply logging on to your mySSA account at SSA.Gov.

Mistakes in an individual's Social Security earnings record are actually much more common than most people think. In tax year 2012 alone, the Social Security Administration reported $71 billion in wages that could not be matched to an individual's earnings record. The good news is that the Social

Security Administration has a system for sorting out some of these mistakes and assigning the earnings to the correct record.

Even so, nearly half of the mismatches are never corrected. That means that in 2012 there was approximately *$35 billion* in wages that was never credited to individual Social Security history.

Why A Social Security Earnings Record Mistake Matters

A mistake in your earnings history can make a big difference in how your Social Security benefits are calculated. How? It all goes back to the benefits formula. We'll cover the formula in the next chapter, but as a summary, you should know that the Social Security Administration uses your highest 35 years of earnings as a cornerstone of the benefit calculation.

If any of these 35 years are incorrect or missing altogether, the average is skewed. One year of missing earnings can make a big difference in the amount of lifetime income you'll receive from Social Security.

Chapter 3 Takeaways

- You can earn up to 4 Social Security credits per year.

- The credit requirements for the various programs are not all the same.

- It is very important to check your earnings history for accuracy every year

Chapter 4

How Your Benefit Is Calculated

It's important for you to have a clear understanding of the process used to calculate your Social Security benefits. If you understand this calculation, you may be able to spot mistakes and fix them before it's too late.

Like anything with Social Security, the rules can seem complex at first. To help you, I distilled several pages of calculation rules into four easy-to-understand steps.

Step 1: Inflation Adjustment

All your earnings through age 59 are adjusted for inflation. This adjustment is simply meant to ensure your Social Security benefit reflects today's cost of living. If your benefit was based on your earnings without that inflation adjustment, it would be much lower. For example, if you turned 62 in 2020. Your prior earnings would be indexed as follows:

Say you earned $10,000 in 1980. The Social Security Administration would multiply that $10,000 in earnings by 4.1671768 to get inflation-adjusted earnings of $41,671.

Then, they would multiply your 1981 earnings by a different number which was established for that year. They would do the same for each year of earnings up to your age 60. The money you earn at age 60 and beyond isn't adjusted for inflation but added to your earnings history at face value.

Don't worry too much about this part of the calculation. You probably won't need to do this on your own, but it's important to understand how your prior benefits are increased to account for inflation.

Step 2: AIME Calculation

Once the SSA inflates your historical earnings to represent today's cost of living, they pick out the highest 35 years. If you have less than 35 years of earnings, the calculation still uses 35 years but will substitute zeros in years where you didn't earn an income. The Administration then adds up all 35 years worth of earnings. Next, since the goal is to obtain a monthly number, they divide the sum by 420 (which is the number of months in 35 years).

The result is the average amount of inflation-adjusted earnings during each month of your highest 35 years of earnings. The Social Security Administration refers to this number as "Average Indexed Monthly Earnings," or more commonly by its acronym, "AIME."

Step 3: Primary Insurance Amount Calculation

The Social Security Administration often uses the acronym "PIA" when referring to your benefit amount. In some places, the SSA also calls it by its full name: the Primary Insurance Amount. The PIA is simply the term for your benefit at your full retirement age (see chapter 5).

Once your average indexed monthly earnings are calculated (your AIME, from above), the SSA uses their formula to calculate your PIA. This is accomplished by calculating your AIME through three separate bands which are in effect in the year you attain age 62:

1. For earnings that fall within the first band, you multiply by 90%. That is the first part of your benefit.

2. For earnings that fall within the second band, you multiply by 32%. That is the second part of your benefit.

3. For earnings that are greater than the maximum of the second band, you multiply by 15%. This is the third part of your benefit.

The sum of these three bands is your benefit amount at full retirement age: your PIA, or Full Retirement Age benefit amount.

You may often see these bands referred to as "Bend Points" if you read the SSA website. If you graphed this formula, you'd see the results appear as a series of line segments joined at these amounts.

If you decide to do this calculation on your own, you should note that the bend point amounts generally change on an annual basis and *ONLY the formula in effect for the year you attain age 62 should be used.*

In the chart below I've illustrated how the formula works for someone who turns 62 in 2021 with an average inflation-adjusted earnings of $6,000 per month.

Social Security Formula 2021				
Your averaged indexed monthly earnings (AIME) AFTER indexing for inflation	2021 Bend Points	Multiplier		Social Security Benefit at Full Retirement Age
	$0 - $996	90%	=	$896 +
$6,000	$997 - $6,002	32%	=	$1,601 +
	>$6,003	15%	=	$0
				= $2,497

You may have noticed that the lower earnings are credited to your benefit amount (PIA) at a higher percentage. This is because the formula, and Social Security in general, is progressive. It was created to provide income for those who truly needed the support. A worker with lower wages might expect to receive a Social Security benefit that replaces up to 90% of his historical earnings, assuming the worker retires at full retirement age. A worker with much higher earnings will receive a larger Social Security benefit, but it may replace only around 25% of lifetime historical earnings.

Chapter 4 Takeaways

- There are three steps in calculating your benefit amount, and the formula gives more weight to lower earnings.

- The Social Security benefit formula considers the highest 35 years of your earnings.

- The "bend point" formula that is used is the one which is current in the year you attain age 62.

Chapter 5

Your Full Retirement Age and Its Impact on Your Benefits

Your full retirement age is the age at which you can begin receiving benefits and receive 100% of your primary insurance amount (PIA), or your full retirement age benefit. Your full retirement age depends on the year of your birth.

For those born between 1943 and 1954, the full retirement age is 66 years old.

If you were born between 1955 and 1960, your full retirement age will be age 66 plus 2 months for every year after 1954.

Born in 1960 or later? Your full retirement age is 67.

BIRTH YEAR	FULL RETIREMENT AGE
1943-1954	66
1955	66 + 2 months
1956	66 + 4 months
1957	66 + 6 months
1958	66 + 8 months
1959	66 + 10 months
1960 & later	67

If you file at your full retirement age, you get full retirement benefits. But you don't have to file on this date. In fact, you can file earlier or later -- but there are some serious consequences to doing so. Here's what you need to know.

Your Filing Age Can Increase or Reduce Your Benefit

If you file at an age other than your full retirement age, your benefit amount will be reduced or increased. Filing earlier than your full retirement age leaves you with a reduced benefit. Filing later, on the other hand, gives you an increased benefit. When you only need to calculate your benefit (not spousal or survivor benefits), the increases and decreases are pretty simple to understand.

Let's examine the increase first. If you wait to file, you'll receive a credit of 8% for every year you delay up until age 70. The Social Security Administration refers to these increases as "delayed retirement credits."

You only get the increase if you file late. If you file *early*, your full retirement age benefit actually drops below what you'd receive at full retirement age. How much your benefit is reduced depends on your age when you file. If you file at 66, just one year early, your benefit will be reduced by almost 7%. If you begin receiving benefits at age 62, your benefit would drop far more dramatically and be 30% lower than what you would receive at your full retirement age.

Social Security Benefit by Filing Age	
62	70%
63	75%
64	80%
65	86%
66	93%
67	100%
68	108%
69	116%
70	124%

Chart Assumes Age 67 is Full Retirement Age

That's a simple overview of the reductions you face for filing early and the increased benefit you'll receive for filing later. But what if you plan to file at 67 years and 8 months? How do the credits – or reductions – break down monthly?

There are three separate calculation bands used to determine how much your benefit will increase or decrease with each month that you file before or after your full retirement age. This calculation can be used no matter what your full retirement age may be.

- .667% Monthly *Increase* – Every month after full retirement age

- .555% Monthly *Decrease* – During the 36-month period prior to full retirement age

- .417% Monthly *Decrease* – Greater than 36 months prior to full retirement age

Monthly Reductions/Increases

(-) .417%	(-) .556%		(+) .667%
More Than 36 Months Before FRA	36 Month Period Before FRA	FULL RETIREMENT AGE	After FRA

In a later chapter, we'll cover how to decide when precisely you should file for Social Security. For now, know that understanding your increases - or reductions - for filing at the various ages is a part of this very important decision.

Chapter 5 Takeaways

- Full retirement age is not the same age for everyone.

- Your benefits will be reduced or increased based on your filing age.

- The increases or reductions occur on a monthly basis.

Chapter 6
The Earnings Limit

At one of my first speaking engagements, I heard a great story from one of the attendees. A few years before, she'd been at her bridge club when the topic turned to Social Security. As they chatted about it, the consensus around the table seemed to be that filing at 62 was the smartest thing to do. This lady, trusting the advice of some of her closest friends, filed for benefits as soon as she turned 62.

She then told me that she'd always wanted to buy a brand-new Toyota Camry. She figured that once she started receiving Social Security income, it would be the perfect time to buy the car. She was still working, which meant her Social Security check would be extra income.

So that's exactly what she did: she bought the car and took out a car loan that she planned to pay with the income from her Social Security benefits.

A few months later, she received a nasty letter from the Social Security Administration stating that she had been paid benefits that she was not eligible for. They asked her to pay the benefits back and informed her that her benefits would be suspended due to her income. Now she had a new car and a car loan, without the Social Security benefits to pay for it.

What happened here? Something that surprises more than just the poor Camry owner who approached me that day: the Social Security earnings limit.

What Is the Social Security Earnings Limit?

The earnings limit is also known as the income limit, the earnings limit, or the earnings test. (The official term is earnings test but income limit and earnings limit are the terms that you'll hear most often.)

Bottom line: they all mean the same thing.

Four quick things before we jump all the way into explaining the test or limit:

1. Be aware that we are talking about Social Security income limits for retirement benefits, not disability or SSI.

2. The earnings limit on Social Security is *not* the same as income taxes on Social Security. Don't get the two confused! We'll cover taxes in a later chapter.

3. The earnings limit does *not* apply if you file for benefits at your full retirement age or beyond. These limits *only apply* to those who begin taking Social Security benefits *before* reaching full retirement age.

4. The earnings limit is an individual limit. If you are still working, and your spouse is drawing Social Security, your earnings will not count towards their income limit.

Why We Have An Earnings Limit

Not long ago, a viewer on my YouTube channel asked me to give her a good reason why we have the Social Security earnings limit. The comments that followed showed how many viewers shared the belief that the earnings limit is unfair and should be eliminated.

In my response, I explained that the rationale behind the entire program of Social Security was a safety net. The original intent of the Social security program was not to supplement retirement income, but to keep the elderly (most of whom lost any potential long-term wealth in the Great Depression) out of poverty.

I also added that today's earnings limit is relatively generous compared to where the Social Security earnings limit began.

The original Economic Security Bill (which is what the Social Security Act was originally called) President Roosevelt sent to Congress featured a very restrictive earnings limit.

It said, *"No person shall receive such old-age annuity unless . . . He is not employed by another in a gainful occupation."*

Whoa! This means that if you had even a single dollar in wages from a job, you could not collect a Social Security benefit at all.

Thankfully, the system we have in place today allows for individuals to have some earnings from work while they are receiving a Social Security benefit. However, it's very important to stay informed on the dollar amount of this limit because it changes every year.

For 2021 the limit is $18,960. For every $2 you exceed that limit, $1 will be withheld in benefits. The exception to this dollar limit is in the calendar year that you will reach full retirement age. For the period between January 1 and the month you attain full retirement age, the income limit increases to $50,5200 (for 2021) without a reduction in benefits. For every $3 you exceed that limit, $1 will be withheld in benefits.

This means that if you have a birthday in July, you'll have 6 months of an increased income limit before it drops completely off at your full retirement age. This increased limit and decreased withholding amount allows many individuals to retire at the beginning of the calendar year in which they attain full retirement age.

Again, once you reach full retirement age, there is no reduction in benefits regardless of your income level.

2021 SOCIAL SECURITY INCOME LIMIT		
AGE	INCOME	WITHHOLDING
Under FRA	$18,960	For every $2 over the limit, $1 is withheld from benefits
In the calendar year FRA is reached	$50,520	For every $3 over the limit, $1 is withheld from benefits until the month of full retirement age
At FRA or older	No limit	None

To put these numbers into context, let's look at an example of how this might work in a real-life scenario.

Rosie is 64 years old. She started taking Social Security benefits as soon as she turned 62. Based on her birth year, her full retirement age is 66. Right now, Rosie is eligible for

$20,000 in Social Security benefits per year. She also worked during the year and made $28,960 in wages.

The question we want to understand is, how much was Rosie's benefit reduced by working while on Social Security? To answer that, we first need to calculate how much Rosie was over the Social Security earnings limit for her age.

In 2020, Rosie filed for Social Security and received her first check in January of 2021. Throughout the year she received $1,667 in benefits every month. Without knowing the rules, she also worked and earned $28,960 in wages. With an earnings limit of $18,960, she was over by $10,000.

$28,960 Total Wages
– $18,960 Social Security Income Limit
$10,000 Income in Excess Of Limit

Because this is a full calendar year during which Rosie is receiving benefits but is not yet full retirement age, the benefits reduction amount is $1 reduction for every $2 in excess wages. Since she was over the limit by $10,000, her benefits will be reduced by $5,000.

The benefit reduction calculation would appear as follows:

$10,000 Income in Excess of Limit
x 50% ($1 reduction for every $2 over limit)
$5,000 Benefit Reduction

With the benefits reduction for exceeding the income limits, Rosie Retiree's $20,000 yearly allowed benefit has been reduced to a $15,000 benefit for the year.

In the following year she would attain her full retirement age and would be subject to a much higher income limit.

Special Rule for the First Year (Grace Year)

Many people who retire mid-year have already earned more income than the limit allows. This is why there is a special rule where the earnings limit switches from an annual limit to a monthly limit. (These monthly limits are 1/12 of the annual limit.)

This rule allows you to receive a check for any month you are considered "retired" by the SSA even if you have already exceeded the annual earnings limit.

The interpretation of "retired" as defined by the SSA can cause some confusion. Here's what they mean by this term. In 2021, you are retired if: Your monthly earnings are $1,580 or less and you did not perform substantial services in self-employment. Essentially, you are considered retired unless you make more than the income limit.

The rule for the year you reach full retirement age also applies when working with the monthly limit. In 2021 the limit is $4,210 (1/12 of $50,520).

It's very important to remember that in the year following this first year, the monthly limit is no longer used and the earnings limit is based solely on your annual earnings limit.

How The Earnings Limit Is Applied

The most confusing part of the benefit reduction due to income is how it's reflected in your monthly benefits deposits. Instead of taking out a little bit every month, the SSA will withhold several months of benefits at a time. If you predict in advance that you will have excess earnings and report this to the Social Security Administration, they may take a few months of benefits before you actually earn the anticipated excess earnings.

For example, if your Social Security payment is $1,667 per month, and you expect to receive $28,960 in wages from your job, the Administration would calculate that you'll be over your earnings limit by $10,000 and thus $5,000 in benefits should be withheld. So, they would withhold your benefit payment from January to March. In April, your checks would resume.

If you don't report excess income before you earn it, then you have to report this information after the fact. You can do this when you file your income tax return, but the preferred method is to be proactive and call your local Social Security Administration office. If you wait for the Social Security Administration to learn of your excess earnings via your tax return, there could be a significant gap between the time you earn the excess income and the time that they withhold your benefits. In most cases, it's better to report the excess earnings quickly so the benefits reduction occurs closer to the time you actually earn that extra income.

Regardless of whether your benefits are withheld in advance or in arrears, benefits withholding can make budgeting and planning difficult, especially if you don't understand the system. You may need to create a separate savings account to set some of those earnings aside to compensate for benefits withholding that will occur in the future.

What Kind of Income Counts as Earnings?

The Social Security income limit applies only to gross wages and net earnings from self-employment. All other income is exempt, including pensions, interest, annuities, IRA distributions and capital gains. The term "wages" refers to your gross wages. This is the money that you earn before any deductions, including taxes, retirement contributions, or other deductions.

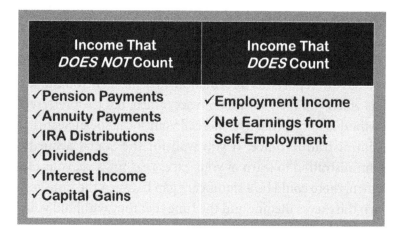

Income That DOES NOT Count	Income That DOES Count
✓Pension Payments ✓Annuity Payments ✓IRA Distributions ✓Dividends ✓Interest Income ✓Capital Gains	✓Employment Income ✓Net Earnings from Self-Employment

What to Do If Your Benefits Are Already Being Withheld

If you're subject to the Social Security earnings limit, don't wait for the SSA to start reducing the benefit you receive. Instead, I'd recommend voluntarily suspending benefits. If you wait for the Social Security Administration to discover that you've earned too much working while receiving benefits, your risk of an overpayment notice is higher.

In any case, if your benefits are withheld because you earned more than the Social Security income limits, don't worry: you aren't missing payments that you'll never get back. Your benefit amount will be recalculated at your full retirement age (or when you stop working) to reflect the months that benefits were withheld.

The best way to avoid the earnings limitation is to wait until full retirement age to file for benefits. If you can't wait, make sure you have a clear understanding of how working impacts your Social Security benefits.

Chapter 6 Takeaways

- There is a limit to the amount you can earn and draw Social Security if you are less than full retirement age and working/earning an income.

- The earnings limit changes in the year you reach your full retirement age.

- There is no income limit once you attain full retirement age.

- Not all income sources are treated as earnings.

Chapter 7
Length of Marriage Rules

If you've had prior marriages, it is crucial to know about the length of marriage rules. The Social Security Administration has separate length of marriage rules for:

- Survivor Benefits

- Spousal Benefits

- Divorced Spouses

Survivor Benefit - *9 Months*
Spouse Benefits - *1 Year*
Divorce Spouse - *10 Years*

The benefit that has the shortest length of marriage requirement is the survivor benefit. It only requires that you were married for nine months before you can file to receive it. There are a few reasons that this rule is waived for surviving spouses. Broadly speaking, it could be waived if:

(a) You are the natural or adoptive parent of the deceased worker's biological child, or (b) if the death was a result of an accident. If one of these exceptions apply to you, the nine-month marriage requirement does not apply.

Spousal benefits are easier to understand. The marriage must have lasted for one continuous year. Simple.

The length of marriage requirement for divorced spouses, on the other hand, is 10 years. The "divorced spouse" category is a little unique in that it is not a category on its own. As a divorced spouse, you may be entitled to either survivor benefits or spousal benefits. The determining factor as to which one you would be eligible for is the status of your ex-spouse. If they are alive, you could be eligible for spousal benefits. If they are deceased, you could be eligible for survivor benefits.

If you remarry prior to age 60, you lose the right to claim on an ex-spouse's record — at least until the subsequent marriage(s) end in death or divorce. If you remarry after age 60, you're eligible to receive benefits based on whatever is highest: your benefit, a spousal benefit on your current spouse's, or a deceased spouse's survivor benefit.

And in the case of multiple marriages? If all marriages have ended, and you've met the length of marriage rules, you can choose the highest benefit from any of your ex-spouses.

Chapter 8

Spousal Benefits

The original Social Security Act provided retirement benefits only to the worker. Spouses were not eligible. In 1939, the law was amended to allow women to collect a spousal benefit. In 1950, men became eligible to draw a spousal benefit. Since then, the spousal benefit has become a very important part of retirement income.

If you're eligible and can qualify, the spousal benefit can be as much as 50% of the higher-earning spouse's full retirement age benefit. If your spouse's full retirement age benefit amounts to $2,000 per month, your spousal benefit at *your* full retirement age could amount to $1,000 per month.

This benefit cannot be more than 50% of the higher-earning spouse's full retirement benefit... but it *can* be less! The benefit is also based on your filing age. Depending on how old you are when you file, the spousal benefit amount will range between 32.5% and 50% of the higher-earning spouse's full retirement benefit.

Check out the chart below to get an idea of how the benefit works and what your payment might be if you can take advantage of spousal benefits. The chart assumes that *your* full retirement age is 67 and your spouse's full retirement age benefit is $2,000 per month.

Your Spouse's Full Retirement Age Benefit Amount	Your Age	% of Your Spouse's FRA Benefit You Will Receive	Your Benefit Amount
$2,000	62	32.50%	$650
$2,000	63	35%	$700
$2,000	64	37.5%	$750
$2,000	65	41.66%	$833
$2,000	66	45.83%	$917
$2,000	67	50%	$1,000

Full Retirement Age is age 66 for those born between 1943 and 1954. Add 2 months for every year thereafter until 1960. After 1960, the FRA is age 67

Did you notice the steep penalty for filing early? You receive significantly less in payments if you choose to file sooner rather than wait until full retirement age.

You may have also noticed that the spousal benefit does *not* increase beyond your full retirement age. When considering your own Social Security benefit, there can be a lot of advantages to waiting to file and delaying when you start receiving payments well past your retirement age, but that's not the case here.

So if a spousal benefit is all that you are entitled to, as we assume in the chart above, there's usually not a good reason to delay filing beyond your personal full retirement age because that won't increase how much you receive.

How to Calculate Your Own Spousal Benefits the Right Way

The spousal benefit calculation is straightforward if you don't have a benefit of your own. Remember, in that case, it's between 32.5% and 50% of the higher-earning spouse's full retirement age benefit, depending on *your* filing age.

However, it can seem a little more complicated if you have Social Security benefits from your work history. And to keep things interesting, the Social Security Administration decided that a *different* calculation method should be used to determine how much each benefit should increase/decrease based on your filing age. As complicated as Social Security benefits can seem, there is a way to correctly calculate how much your spousal benefit will be if you qualify to receive it.

Your Own Benefit Reduction/Increase	Your Age	Spousal Benefit Reduction/Increase
70%	62	65%
75%	63	70%
80%	64	75%
86.66%	65	83.33%
93.33%	66	91.67%
100%	67	100%
108%	68	100%
116%	69	100%
124%	70	100%

Full Retirement Age is age 66 for those born between 1943 and 1954. Add 2 months for every year thereafter until 1960. After 1960, the FRA is age 67

If you understand how they break down the individual benefits, it's not hard to use the table above to quickly figure out what your approximate benefit will be. Here's an example.

Joe and Julie each have a Social Security benefit from work they individually performed. Julie's benefit at her full retirement age is $800 per month. Joe's benefit at his full retirement age is $2,000. Assuming they are both full retirement age when they file, Joe will be entitled to a benefit of $2,000 and Julie will be entitled to the greater of her own benefit **or up to** half of Joe's benefit.

Since half of his is **greater** than her own individual benefit ($1,000 vs. $800), she will receive $1,000 per month. This scenario is simple, but when it comes to calculating different age combinations, it's crucial to understand that Julie will always receive her own benefit amount first and then receive a "spousal top-off" to get her benefit to half of Joe's.

Julie's own benefit, and the benefit she'd get if Joe's benefit was greater, gets treated to a different calculation with regard to how they are increased or decreased based on filing age.

Julie's FRA Benefit
-$800

Joe's FRA Benefit
-$2,000

½

=

$800 + $200 'Spousal Top-Off' = $1,000

For example, if Julie filed at 62, her $800 benefit would be reduced to $560. The $200 "spousal top-off" would be reduced from $200 to $130. As per the chart above, the reduction from $200 to $130 is due to Julie's own benefit being reduced to 70% because she filed early -- so her spousal portion is reduced to 65%. In this scenario, her combined benefit would be $690.

The spousal top-off is only available once the higher earning spouse files for his/her own benefit. This means that if Julie files for her own benefit, but Joe does not, Julie would only be entitled to the benefit on her own work record. Once Joe filed, she would begin receiving the additional spousal top-off benefit.

It's also important for planning to understand that the spousal benefit would be reduced (or not) based on the age of entitlement to that benefit. This means that Julie's reduction to her own benefit would be based on her age when she filed for her benefit. However, her reduction to the spousal benefit would be based on her age when Joe filed for his benefit.

So, if Julie filed when she was 62, her own benefit would be reduced. If she was 67 when Joe finally got around to filing, her spousal top-off would not be reduced.

Divorced? Know This Significant Exception to the Rule

When planning your Social Security filing strategy, it's important to note that you cannot file for a spousal benefit until the higher earning spouse files for their benefit. But this doesn't apply if you are filing for a spousal benefit from an ex-spouse.

If your ex-spouse has not applied for retirement benefits you can receive benefits on his or her record if you have been divorced for at least two years and your ex-spouse is at least 62 years old.

The Two Exceptions to Know About the 1 Year Marriage Requirement

Normally, you must be married for at least 12 continuous months to meet the spousal benefit duration-of-marriage requirement. However, there are two exceptions to this rule.

If you marry someone who is the natural mother or father of your child, the one-year requirement is waived.

Here's how the Social Security Administration puts it: *"Be the natural mother or father of the worker's biological son or daughter; i.e., this requirement is met if a live child was born to the number-holder and claimant although the child need not be alive."*

The 1-year requirement is also waived if you were entitled (or potentially entitled!) to Social Security benefits on someone else's work record in the month before you were married. An example of these benefits would be spousal benefits, survivor benefits or parent's benefits.

For example, let's assume you will be eligible for a spousal benefit from your ex-husband Joe. If you remarry, you wouldn't have to wait the full 12 months to get a spousal benefit from your new spouse. Instead, you'd be immediately eligible.

Hopefully, this chapter helps illustrate the importance of *fully* understanding all your options when it comes to Social Security -- and there are a lot of options to choose from. If you file early, you generally don't get a second chance. And remember, the average retired family receives 38% of their income from Social Security benefits, so it can cost you quite a bit to leave money on the table here.

Chapter 8 Takeaways

- There are different length of marriage rules for different benefit types.

- Spousal benefits are up to 50% of the higher earning spouse's benefit.

- The higher earning spouse must first file in order to trigger eligibility for a spousal benefit.

- When filing at separate times and ages, the benefit can get a little complicated.

Chapter 9
Survivor Benefits

Social Security survivor benefits might be the one thing about Social Security that I can give a simple answer to. If you're wondering whether or not you qualify to receive them, here's how to tell.

At the death of the first spouse, surviving spouses are eligible to receive the higher of:

- Their own monthly benefit, *or*

- The monthly benefit of the deceased.

That's the clean and straightforward answer -- but of course, it's not quite that simple in real life. Every family is different. Unique situations and variables can introduce some complexity. Here's all the other information you need to know to better understand how survivor benefits work, starting with the fact that Social Security pays out two types of benefits upon death. The first is a lump sum death benefit. The second is the monthly survivor benefit.

Lump Sum Death Benefit

Upon the death of a Social Security beneficiary, the Social Security Administration pays a lump-sum death payment of $255. Obviously, a one-time $255 payment doesn't quite cover the cost of a funeral. It's been stuck at that level for several years and inflation has significantly eroded its useful value, so it is no longer called the funeral benefit. It's now officially referred to as the lump sum death benefit.

There are three categories of people who may receive a lump sum death benefit from Social Security:

1. A surviving spouse, who was residing with the deceased spouse, *or*

2. A surviving spouse, who was not residing with the deceased, but was receiving benefits based upon the work record of the deceased spouse, or who becomes eligible for benefits after the death of the spouse, *or*

3. A surviving child, who was receiving benefits based on the work records of the deceased parent, or who became eligible for the benefit after the death of the parent. The payment is divided evenly among all eligible children.

If the eligible spouse or child is not receiving benefits at the time of death, they may receive the benefit if they apply for benefits within two years of the death. If there are no eligible survivor in either of these three categories, then the SSA does not pay a lump sum death benefit.

Determining Eligibility for Monthly Survivor Benefits

Many surviving spouses are eligible for monthly benefits from Social Security, based on their age, disability, children at home, or some combination of these qualifying factors. In general, spouse survivor benefits are available to:

- *Surviving spouses*, who were married at least 9 months, beginning at age 60. Benefit amount may depend on the age at which you file for benefits. Note: the 9-month marriage requirement does not apply if the surviving spouse is the parent of the deceased spouse's natural minor child or if the death was a result of an accident. There are a few other exceptions, but these are the most common.

- *Disabled surviving spouses*, who were married at least 9 months, beginning at age 50. Benefit amount may depend on the age at which you file for benefits. Note: many of the same exceptions generally apply with respect to the 9-month length of marriage requirement as they do to traditional non-disability survivor benefits.

- Surviving spouses, of any age, caring for the deceased's child aged 16 or younger or disabled.

- Former spouses, who were married at least 10 years, beginning at age 60.

Calculating Your Benefit Amount

Figuring out how much you'll receive in Social Security survivor benefits requires a little math.

The simple explanation is that at the death of the first spouse, surviving spouses receive the higher of their own benefit or the benefit of the deceased. But this simple explanation doesn't consider (a) what age the deceased filed for benefits (if they did at all) and (b) when the surviving spouse decides to file.

If the Deceased Did *Not* File for Benefits

If the deceased spouse never filed for benefits, but died on or before their full retirement age, the calculation is relatively easy. The survivor receives the deceased's full retirement age benefit, adjusted for the survivor's filing age.

If the deceased spouse never filed for benefits, and died after their full retirement age, the survivor receives the deceased's benefit in the same amount it would have been on the date of the deceased's death (including delayed retirement credits) reduced for the filing age of the survivor. You can see the next chart for more information on age-based reductions that come into play in both cases.

But what if the deceased spouse filed for benefits before he passed away? If this is the case, it could get a little more confusing.

If the Deceased *Did* File for Benefits

If the deceased spouse filed for benefits on or after their full retirement age, and the surviving spouse is at full retirement age, the benefit amount payable to the survivor will remain unchanged. If the surviving spouse is less than full retirement age, the amount the deceased spouse was receiving would be reduced by the filing age of the survivor.

If the deceased filed for benefits before their full retirement age, the surviving spouse is entitled to the full retirement age benefit of the deceased (reduced for survivor's filing age) but will always be limited to the larger of the actual benefit of the deceased *or* 82.5% of the deceased's PIA.

This 82.5% limit is a special rule often called the "Widows Limit" but the technical name is the RIB-LIM. It's meant to offer some protection for surviving spouses when the deceased spouse filed at, or near, the earliest age possible. This rule states that if your deceased spouse filed early, you'll be forever limited to either the amount they were drawing, or 82.5% of their full retirement age benefit. This rule has been a real lifesaver for some widows and widowers.

When It Doesn't Pay to Delay

Here's where this gets really interesting. If your deceased spouse filed early for benefits, and you are also under full retirement age, there may be no reason to delay your filing beyond a certain age. It may be possible that your survivor benefit will not increase beyond your age 62 and 9 months!

For example, let's assume Jim's full retirement age benefit was $2,000. However, he filed at 62 and began receiving an age-based reduced benefit of $1,500. He died two years later. Because of his early filing, the *most* his surviving spouse, Donna, will receive is the greater of his actual benefit ($1,500) or 82.5% of his full retirement age benefit ($2,000 x 82.5% = $1,650).

Based on the reductions for her filing age, she'd hit the 82.5% ($1,650) of his benefit right in between age 62 and 63. Once Donna was at this age, there would be no benefit to continuing to delay filing for benefits. Further delay wouldn't increase her survivor benefit.

FILING AGE	SURVIVOR BENEFIT REDUCTION OR INCREASE %
50-59	71.50%*
60	71.50%
61	75.58%
62	79.65%
63	83.72%
64	87.79%
65	91.86%
66	95.93%
67	100%**
68	100%
69	100%
70	100%

*Only disabled individuals can file for Survivor benefits as early as age 50. For non-disabled individuals the earliest age is 60.
**Assuming Full Retirement Age is 67.

Full Retirement Age for Survivors Benefits

If you were born before 1962, you need to understand that the definition of "full retirement age" is different for survivor benefits than it is for all other benefits.

Knowing exactly when you are full retirement age is important when filing for your survivor benefits. Why? Because if the survivor benefit is the highest benefit you'll be entitled to, there is generally no benefit to delaying your filing beyond that age.

Several years ago, the Social Security Administration announced that an individual's full retirement age would gradually increase from age 66 to age 67. Since they aren't content with keeping things simple, they decided that the full retirement age for purposes of a survivor benefit would change on a different schedule than it does for everyone else. The chart below has the years of birth and the corresponding full retirement ages.

FULL RETIREMENT AGE BY BIRTH YEAR

SURVIVOR BENEFITS		ALL OTHER BENEFITS	
1945-1956	66	1943-1954	66
1957	66 and 2 months	1955	66 and 2 months
1958	66 and 4 months	1956	66 and 4 months
1959	66 and 6 months	1957	66 and 6 months
1960	66 and 8 months	1958	66 and 8 months
1961	66 and 10 months	1959	66 and 10 months
1962 and later	67	1960 and later	67

Advanced Filing Strategies for Survivors

In early 2018 the Office of the Inspector General released a report with some shocking news. 82% of widows and widowers who are receiving Social Security survivor benefits are actually entitled to a higher monthly benefit payment. The only problem is, the SSA never made them aware of this. This affected an estimated 9,224 widows and widowers 70 and older who could have received an additional $131.8 million in Social Security benefits.

This is because the widow(er)s were never told that they could still use the filing strategies that were now off limits for everyone else.

Prior to 2016, there were several popular Social Security filing strategies that would allow an individual to file for certain benefits and later switch back to their own benefits. This allowed their own benefit to grow with the 8% per year delayed retirement credits (from chapter five). However, law changes in 2016 did away with many of the Social Security filing strategies. But survivors can still use a very powerful filing strategy to maximize their benefit. Here's how it works.

If you have a benefit based on your own work history, it could make sense to file for a reduced survivor benefit as early as 60. While you are drawing your survivor benefit, your own benefit grows every month you delay filing for it. Generally, these adjustments could grow your benefit by 77% from age 62 to age 70. At age 70, you simply switch back to your own benefit (which is now higher).

Now, let us use an example to illustrate this. Say Paula has her own benefit of $1,500 per month that she could take at 67, her full retirement age. Her husband passed away and she is eligible for a survivor benefit of $1,200 per month. If she restricts her application to a survivor benefit only, she can collect benefits while letting her own benefit grow.

From age 62 to 69, she could receive $1,200 per month as a survivor benefit. Once her own benefit has grown to the maximum, at age 70 and beyond, she can simply take that and receive $1,860 per month for the rest of her life.

How to Claim Survivors Benefits

To begin receiving survivor benefits, you must make a claim with the Social Security Administration. You cannot make these online, but you can start the claims process over the telephone by calling 1-800-772-1213. Making an appointment at a local office can help reduce your wait time as well.

A death should be reported to the Social Security Administration as soon as possible. In many cases, the funeral home can make that notification. You will have to provide the funeral home with the deceased's Social Security number.

Documents Required to File Your Claim

The Social Security claims process may require the following documents. You might not need every single piece of paperwork listed here, but it's easier to come prepared than to have to make several trips or follow-up appointments.

- Proof of death—either from a funeral home or death certificate

- Your Social Security number, as well as the deceased's social security number

- Your birth certificate

- Your marriage certificate, if you are a widow or widower

- Dependent children's Social Security numbers, if available, and their birth certificates

- Deceased worker's W-2 forms or federal self-employment tax return for the most recent year

- The name of your bank and your account number so your benefits can be deposited directly into your account.

If you don't have all the documents you need, start the claims process anyway. In many cases, your local Social Security office can contact your state Bureau of Vital Statistics and verify your information online at no cost to you.

Chapter 9 Takeaways

- Survivors benefits can be up to the full benefit of the deceased spouse.

- The widow's limit is 82.5% of the deceased spouse's full retirement age benefit.

- Surviving spouses can still use strategies for filing that are no longer available for everyone else.

Chapter 10

Paying Taxes on Social Security

Paying income taxes on Social Security benefits can be a big shock. I clearly remember it was one of my dad's biggest retirement surprises. Like a lot of other retirees, he didn't know that up to 85% of his Social Security benefit could be counted as taxable income. Ultimately, we were able to mitigate some of his tax burden, but he still owed on other parts of the income. My dad didn't like that one bit, and he's not alone. Every year, individuals retire and are faced with sticker shock when they find out how much they'll have to pay in taxes on Social Security income.

To some, it doesn't seem fair. You've worked for years and paid your Social Security tax as the admission ticket to a Social Security benefit. Now that you're collecting that benefit, you have to pay taxes? Again?

It wasn't always this way, but it all changed with the passage of 1983 Amendments to the Social Security Act. Under this new rule, up to 50% of Social Security benefits were taxable for certain individuals. 10 years later, the Deficit Reduction Act of 1993 expanded the taxation of Social Security benefits.

Under this Act, an additional bracket was added, in which up to 85% of Social Security benefits could be taxable above certain thresholds.

The combination of these laws left us with the current tax structure on Social Security benefits. Today, somewhere between 0% and 85% of your Social Security payment will be included as taxable income. Your Social Security benefit will never be 100% taxable. The maximum amount of benefits that can be included as income is 85%.

To determine how much of your Social Security benefits will be taxable, you first must calculate "provisional income" – a measurement of income used specifically for this purpose. Provisional income can be roughly calculated as your total income from taxable sources, plus any tax-exempt interest (such as interest from tax-free bonds), plus any excluded foreign income, plus 50% of your Social Security benefits.

PROVISIONAL INCOME

Adjusted gross income

+ Tax Exempt Income

+ Excluded Foreign Income

+ 50% of Social Security Benefit

= Provisional Income

Once you've calculated your "provisional income" you can apply it to the threshold tables to determine what percentage of your Social Security will be included as taxable income.

If your total "provisional income" is less than $32,000 ($25,000 if single), none of your Social Security benefits will be taxable. However, once your total exceeds $32,000 ($25,000 for singles), then part of your benefits become taxable as income.

Take this example to help you better understand how this works:

Tim and Donna recently retired. They own some rental property that generates about $12,000 in net annual income. Their combined Social Security benefit is $3,000 per month, or $36,000 per year. In addition to this income, they plan to take an annual distribution from their IRA in the amount of $32,000.

Using the income from those sources, here's how the provisional income would be calculated.

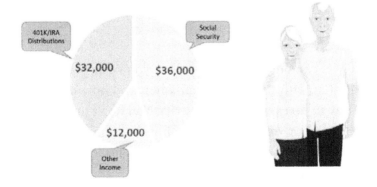

$18,000 (½ of Social Security benefits)
+$32,000 401K/IRA Distributions
<u>+$12,000 Other Income</u>
$62,000 Provisional Income

Now that we know Tim and Donna's provisional income is calculated, we can determine how much of their Social Security benefit is taxable. Based on a married couple with a provisional income of $62,000, it's now a simple matter of applying the income to the thresholds.

The first $32,000 of the provisional income has no impact on whether a Social Security benefit is taxable. 50% of the amounts between $32,000 and $44,000 will be added. 85% of the amount in excess of $44,000 will be added. As a rough calculation, a married couple with a provisional income of $62,000 would have $21,300 of taxable Social Security income.

MARRIED, FILING JOINTLY	% OF BENEFITS ARE TAXABLE	$62,000 PROVISIONAL INCOME	$ AMOUNT OF TAXABLE SOCIAL SECURITY INCOME
$0-$32k	0%	$32,000	$0
Above $32k	50%	$12,000	$6,000
Above $44k	85%	$18,000	$15,300
			TOTAL - $21,300

Since you can only spend the dollars you keep, you need to be familiar with the rules about when and how much you may pay in taxes on Social Security. You don't have to be a tax expert, but you should know how to roughly calculate the amount of taxable Social Security benefits. (For anything deeper, see your tax advisor.)

Taxes on Social Security income shouldn't be a surprise at retirement time, and they can sometimes be avoided or reduced by certain planning strategies. For example, what if Tim and Donna had taken a larger distribution from their retirement accounts in the years prior to claiming their benefit (up until age 70)?

At that point, they could turn on the Social Security benefits which have increased for the delayed filing. With the increased amount of income from Social Security, they could then decrease their distributions from their retirement accounts. Since the provisional income calculation only includes 50% of Social Security, their overall taxable income should be lower for the remainder of their retirement.

That's just one example of how you could strategically tap into your various retirement income sources to maximize your net retirement income. However, strategies like this don't work for everyone. If you need specialized advice, see a knowledgeable financial advisor and work with a tax professional. By building this team, you can see your specific situation from all angles and make the best decisions possible.

Chapter 10 Takeaways

- Social Security benefits may be taxable income.

- Up to 85% of your benefit can be taxed.

- The "provisional income" calculation only includes 50% of your Social Security benefit, but 100% of all your other income.

- There may be strategies to lower the amount of taxes on your Social Security benefit.

Chapter 11
Choosing When to File

The "what's the best age to file for Social Security?" question is the number-one question people ask me about the topic. And it's little wonder because the answer is anything but simple or straightforward. In fact, finding the right answer for *you* often requires a lot of complex thinking and calculating to determine exactly what you should do.

Even if you can manage to do the proper planning on your own, then you're left with an almost-bigger challenge: feeling *confident* that you got the right answer. You can do the hard work of making your best estimate… only to spend a lot of time and energy worrying and second-guessing yourself. So let's get to the bottom of this and to an answer you can use.

When Should You File for Social Security?

At the end of the day, when you should file for Social Security is a highly personal decision that depends on a number of individual factors unique to your situation, life, and finances. But still, it helps to have some guidelines. Thankfully, some common sense knowledge of financial and retirement planning can paint a pretty clear picture to answer the question of when is *best* to file.

If you have adequate retirement savings and a good handle on your retirement expenses, it generally makes sense for at least one person to delay filing if you're married. But according to a recent report from the Center for Retirement Research at Boston College, around 60% of Americans begin collecting Social Security retirement benefits before full retirement age. Nearly half began at 62, which is the earliest age possible to file for benefits.

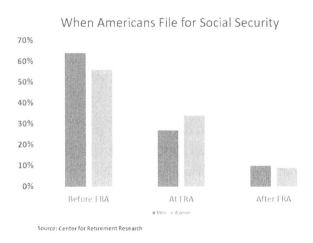

When Americans File for Social Security

Source: Center for Retirement Research

There's *no way* that filing at the earliest age possible was the right strategy for nearly half of all 62-year-olds. So why do so many people file so early for Social Security? Many people make these poor choices in their filing decisions because of something called hyperbolic discounting.

Hyperbolic discounting is a cognitive bias which leads individuals to accept a smaller reward *today* instead of waiting for a known larger reward *later*. This bias becomes stronger when the reward is closer to us (as opposed to farther into the future).

Imagine you are offered $50 today or $60 a week from now. Research around hyperbolic discounting usually finds that most individuals would choose the $50 today. But when the option is to wait 52 weeks to get $50 or wait 53 weeks to get $60, most choose to wait the 53 weeks for the higher reward. The behavioral thought is, "I'm already waiting a year; what's another week?"

Hyperbolic discounting is easy to observe in retirement planning. You can build the perfect retirement plan with an optimal retirement income strategy. The client, when they're still in the middle of their career, agrees that filing at a certain age is best.

But as clients begin to approach age 62, they start to waver on that initial decision (which was strategic and logical). Often, they just file as soon as they turn 62 due to the hyperbolic discounting bias that leads to illogical, irrational decision-making.

When someone is offered $1,540 per month today or $2,728 per month starting in eight years, it's just too tempting to start accepting the money today instead of waiting.

We'd all like to believe that we make decisions based on the facts and not emotions. When it gets right down to it, though, our emotions can and often do take over. That leads to decision-making that doesn't provide the optimal outcome, and it's why so many people file too early for Social Security benefits.

So how do you overcome this challenge?

Using a Break-even Analysis? Stop! Read This First

You should arm yourself with the facts on who should file, and when, if you want to know the right steps that you need to take. But before we can get into what the best age for filing is for you, we need to talk about why you must *avoid* using a break-even analysis.

For years, this was the preferred method of identifying the 'right' age to file. At one time, the Social Security Administration had a break-even analysis on their website! Thankfully, they've since taken it down. This old-school approach to figuring out when to file only takes into consideration *your* life expectancy and completely ignores the other factors that should be part of a filing decision.

A break-even analysis simply compares your total cumulative lifetime benefits amounts for filing at various ages. For example, if you started collecting benefits at an earlier date, and die before reaching the break-even age, you come out ahead. If you live beyond your break-even age, you would have been better off to have filed later.

Check out the chart below. You'll see that age 78 is the 'break-even' between filing at 62 vs. 67. In other words, it's this point when you would have been better off to have waited until 67 to have filed. If you died before 78, you would have been better off filing at 62. In comparing age 67 vs. 70, you would have to live past age 82 for it to be beneficial to have filed at 70.

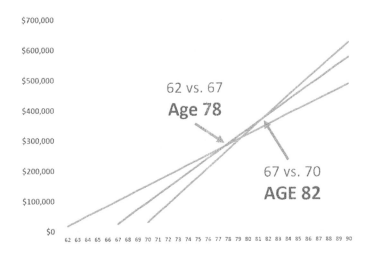

The question that the break-even analysis answers is, "What if I die early?" This question is such a small part of the filing decision. It only considers *your* benefit amount and completely ignores the optimization of spousal and survivor benefits and the role your benefit amount may play in their lifetime.

A real analysis to determine your filing strategy should not only consider what happens if you were to pass away, but also ask the question, "What if I live longer than expected?"

What Is the Best Age for *You* to File for Social Security?

To further help you understand when it's best to file, let's look at some different scenarios and what each case means for determining whether to file early, at retirement, or later.

When You Should File Early for Social Security

Although it's less common, filing early *can* be the best strategy for some people. Bear in mind that even if one of these scenarios aligns with your own, filing early may not be an option if you're still working. Remember that the Social Security Administration has an earnings limit that is applied if you are less than full retirement age and working while collecting benefits.

Here are a few cases where it *could* make sense.

You need the income

There's not much strategy here. If you need the income because of a job loss or some other factor, you need to go file -- unless the income deficit is coming from a disability. In that case, check your eligibility status for Social Security disability.

It might make more sense to file for disability instead of retirement benefits. The retirement benefit is 70% of your full retirement age benefit. The disability payment is 100% of your full retirement age payment.

So how do you know if you are eligible for Social Security Disability? Chapter 3 covered this in more detail, but this is what you should know as a summary. There are specific work requirements that the Social Security Administration has for qualifying. Unlike a retirement benefit, where you can qualify for benefits and then not participate for several decades, the disability benefit requires you to be "currently insured." In addition to requiring 40 credits, you must also have recent work history. In fact, 20 of your credits must have earned in the last 10 years ending with the year you become disabled.

There are exceptions to the qualifications for disability. I would highly encourage you to seek the counsel of an attorney who practices in this area if you feel you may qualify.

You have minor or disabled children

If you have children (or eligible grandchildren) or a spouse providing care for these children at home, they may be eligible for benefits. You'll have to file first, though. This is because a rule that states that before benefits can be paid to anyone off of your work history, you have to be receiving benefits.

When combined with your benefit, the benefits to children and your eligible spouse can be up to 180% of your full retirement age benefit. So if you have children at home that meet the criteria, there's an obvious reason to consider filing early.

You are the lower earner and your spouse is in poor health

If your spouse had higher earnings than you, their benefit will be higher than yours. If they are also in poor health with a shortened life expectancy, it's likely that your benefit will terminate and you'll simply begin receiving their benefit as a survivor.

Your spouse is the lower earner *and* older than you

If your spouse is older than you, and their own benefit is not as high as the amount they can receive as a spousal benefit, it could make sense to file and open up your work record to pay a spousal benefit. When you compare the total amount of benefits you both could receive, this strategy could make more sense than you delaying your own.

When You Should File Later for Social Security

Absent one of the factors where it makes sense to file for a benefit early, you probably just need to file later. Then the question becomes, how *much* later? Again, that depends on your unique situation, but one thing should be clear: retiring and filing for Social Security *do not* have to happen at the same time. It may be optimal for you to file for benefits years before, or after, you leave work.

If you're still thinking about filing early, without one of the aforementioned reasons, here are a few other things to think about.

The return is good (really good)

Imagine you heard about an income-producing investment backed by the US government. They're willing to pay you today, but they have a special deal for you to consider. If you just delay receiving payments for 8 years, they'll increase your lifetime monthly benefit payment by as much as 77%.

Do you think you'd be interested?

That's exactly what you can enjoy when you delay your Social Security benefit. If you wait to file for Social Security until age 70, your benefit will be 77% higher. This fantastic increase in benefits is often underestimated by individuals who file early for benefits even if they don't need the income. They'll often file and then just let the monthly checks pile up in their bank account. I'll bet that bank account won't increase by 77% in 8 years.

You could lower your overall tax bill in retirement

Although this was mentioned in Chapter 9, it bears revisiting in this context. Somewhere between 0% and 85% of your Social Security benefits will be added to your taxable income. It could make sense to delay filing to reduce these taxes in retirement. This won't work for everyone, but for those in the right income bracket, it could make a big difference.

In order to determine how much of your benefit will be taxable, you first have to calculate "provisional income" – a measurement of income used specifically for this purpose. Provisional income can be roughly calculated as your total income from taxable sources, plus any tax-exempt interest (such as interest from tax-free bonds), plus any excluded foreign income, plus 50% of your Social Security benefits.

Assume that you need $5,000 per month in income. Your Social Security benefit at your full retirement age is $1,000 and you have a pension of $3,000. So you have income sources of $4,000 and a need of $5,000. Imagine that you plan to fill this $1,000 shortfall with a distribution from a retirement account.

What if you delayed your Social Security until you reach age 70? You'd have to take $2,000 per month from your retirement accounts, but then you could switch on your Social Security benefit at 70 which would be $1,240.

Now you only need $760 in monthly distributions from your retirement accounts to meet your shortfall. And since only half of your Social Security is counted in the provisional income calculation, the overall provisional income should be reduced. That results in less of your benefit being taxed.

All this being said, your tax advisor is the best resource for recommendations on a tax plan for retirement and Social Security, so be sure to touch base with them and talk through the specifics of your situation before making a final decision based on tax benefits.

Chapter 11 Takeaways

- There is no single best age to file. There are great reasons to file early, and great reasons to file later. Everyone's situation is different.

Chapter 12
How to Find Help

Getting answers to your Social Security questions can be really difficult. I've talked to many individuals who have nearly given up in frustration and just accepted what they were being told (even if it didn't make sense).

This guide is a good place to start, but you likely need to rely on other resources to get you all the way through the process with success and no mistakes. If you know where (and how) to look for help, your chances of getting your questions answered should be much better.

Here are the places you can go to, in order of where you should start.

The Social Security Administration Offices

The Social Security Administration may be the most obvious choice for assistance with Social Security questions, but it's not always the easiest place to get answers. After several phone calls and visits, you may give up in frustration. While your experience may differ, I've found the Social Security technicians to be a mixed bag. Some are brilliant and know more than I have ever will. However, there are some who know very little about the program.

If you want to increase your chances of finding someone who knows a lot about the program, you need to understand the hierarchy within your local Social Security office. Not all employees have the same level of knowledge and experience. For retirement and disability benefits, the Social Security employee you speak to when you go to an office or call will most likely have one of the following titles:

- **Service Representative:** These employees have the responsibility of handling general inquiries, fixing simple post-claim issues and answering the phones. Simply put, they are the generalists in the office. Although this is the first position for a new hire, I wouldn't automatically discount their experience. Some Service Representatives begin, and end, a long Social Security career with the same title.

- **Claims Representative:** This employee is there for one reason: to assist individuals in filing claims for benefits under Social Security programs. Unless you are ready to process your claim, you'll have little interaction with this representative.

- **Technical Experts**: These employees handle complex cases and stuff that's too complicated for most of the other workers in the office. Technical experts I've communicated with have exhibited a deep understanding of the rules and provisions of the Social Security programs. But you won't find them answering the phones or meeting with just anyone. Normally, you must be referred by a Service Representative or a Claims Representative to get in front of the Technical Expert.

The next time you call (or visit) your local Social Security office, you'll speak to a Service Representative. Give them a chance and they may be able to help you. However, if you have *any* doubt about what you're being told, it's time to escalate. Ask them to let you speak to a Technical Expert. It may take a while, but eventually, you'll be able to speak to the most knowledgeable person in the office.

Attorneys

If you've exhausted your options at the Social Security office, you may want to try to find a Social Security disability attorney to help you. Although they generally practice specifically in the area of disability benefits, they are usually well versed in the entire program.

But you may get frustrated here as well. Most of these attorneys can help you with your Social Security questions, but you may have to look around for a while. Why? The attorneys that work with Social Security disability benefits are accustomed to being compensated on a contingency model. If they win a disability case, they are paid a portion of the past due disability benefits. If no past due benefits are awarded, the attorney will not receive a fee.

So the first thing you'll have to do is ask them if they would be willing to help you on an hourly basis. You may have to call a few before you'll find one to agree to this, but eventually, you will find the right fit.

Financial Planners

Although it seems that it should be easy, finding a financial planner who deeply understands Social Security can be tough. There are no legitimate education programs that teach financial planners what they need to know in order to help clients with Social Security, so you can't look for a specific certification or designation.

It's up to you to find out if a particular planner is passionate enough about the topic to have sought out and developed specialized knowledge in this area, and taken the time required to learn all the ins and outs of Social Security and the filing rules. There's only one way to do that. You need to ask lots of questions!

One of the first questions you should ask is, "Do you offer financial planning on an hourly basis?" This is the only way I would consider engaging someone to help you. If they say they don't charge anything and will help you with your planning for free, there's a strong likelihood that's because a sales pitch for a financial product like insurance or annuities is coming at some point during the process of "helping" you.

Once you find a planner who will help you on an hourly basis, it's time to find out what they know about Social Security. A good question to get started with would be the very one we sought to address here: "What's the best age to file?"

What you're hoping to hear is not some rule of thumb answer (like, "67 years old"). They should ask you a few follow-up questions that will help them determine the specifics of your situation. If they give you an easy rule-of-thumb answer, they *don't* know Social Security beyond a surface level.

If they do okay with that question, here are a few more questions you can ask:

- What is my full retirement age?

- How much will my benefits increase between age 62 and my full retirement age?

- What are the length of marriage rules?

- How does work affect my benefit?

- Can you explain provisional income?

These are very basic questions that any financial planner with competency in Social Security will be comfortable and confident in answering immediately. If they can't, keep looking! If you are diligent in your search, you'll find the help you need.

Chapter 12 Takeaways

- Finding the help you need is possible if you understand:

  - the hierarchy of support at your local Social Security office

  - how to approach compensation with an attorney

  - the questions to ask a financial planner to ensure they are qualified to assist you with Social Security

Chapter 13
Conclusion

Whether your retirement is in the future, or you're living there now, I'm glad you've decided to read this guide to the Social Security essentials. Hopefully, I'll leave you with something that will help you to have a more successful and prosperous retirement.

As you may have already discovered, a successful retirement doesn't just happen on its own. It takes careful planning and plenty of self-education. You can have the greatest financial, tax and legal advisors, but none of them will feel the pain and regret of big retirement mistakes like you will. On that note, I'd like to cover a broader retirement planning topic before we conclude this book.

Several years ago, I was talking to a friend about the typical retirement plan. He is an estate planning and elder law attorney and was seeing the same problems I saw each day in my financial planning practice. Clients would begin the process of retirement and get misguided advice from their financial planner, attorney, or accountant.

It's not that the advice was bad on its own, but it was offered without consideration of all of the other factors. It's as if the client's advisory team all set up offices on individual islands with no communication to the other islands. This is a recipe for disaster!

I had one case where a client retired and needed to invest a large sum of money from the sale of his business. When I visited with him, I noticed that he was unusually adamant about putting it all in tax-free bonds. He told me that his accountant told him he should only buy tax-free bonds. The problem was, he had other issues that posed a serious conflict with this strategy.

First, most of his investable funds were held inside of an irrevocable trust that had been set up by his attorney. The structure of this trust would only allow the distribution of interest income, meaning that he needed to generate significant income outside the trust. A portfolio of tax-free bonds would have only generated a fraction of what he needed. For the rest of his income, he would have been forced to liquidate some of his bonds. This would not only have grave consequences for the trust structure but could place the client in the position of selling bonds at the wrong time. This recommendation didn't consider the client's unique legal position.

Second, tax-free bonds were seriously overpriced at the time. Buying bonds at that time would have almost certainly meant a loss within a one to two year period. There were other asset classes that simply made more sense right then, even if the trust was not an issue.

In this case, the accountant's advice was only good from a tax perspective. It didn't work with either the client's financial plan or their legal plan. It wasn't bad advice, but it was bad advice for this client because it didn't consider their unique situation.

Advice without a big picture perspective is certainly not limited to accountants. I've seen lots of bad advice given by financial planners and attorneys as well. Don't let this happen to you! You need to hire an advisory team that will work together and communicate for the proper integration of your financial, tax and legal planning.

This is achievable. You just need to find the right fit.

Ask your attorney who they use most often for tax advice and financial planning. Then ask your tax advisor who they turn to for legal advice and financial planning. Finally, ask your financial advisor who they use for tax advice and legal work.

It's likely you'll start to hear some of the same people mentioned by the various professionals. This could be the start of your advisory team. Don't be intimidated by these professionals or be afraid to ask them tough questions. Remember, this is *your* retirement, so take charge!

Again, I congratulate you for picking up this book and making it to the conclusion.

You can always find me at Socialsecurityintelligence.com where I'll be researching and simplifying the crazy Social Security rules and cheering you on as you navigate the maze of retirement planning and all the complex, nuanced topics that come with it.

Made in the USA
Monee, IL
28 November 2022

18811541R00066